Mama, Who Is Jesus?

Andrea L. Walker

Illustrated by Titus Rowell

Los Angeles   California

Copyright © 2015 by Andrea L. Walker
Los Angeles, California
All rights reserved
Printed and Bound in the United States of America

Published And Distributed By
Create Noise Publishing
Los Angeles, California
Createnoise1@gmail.com

Packaging/Consulting
Professional Publishing House
1425 W. Manchester Ave. Ste B
Los Angeles, California 90047
323-750-3592
Email: professionalpublishinghouse@yahoo.com
www.Professionalpublishinghouse.com

Cover design: TWA Solutions
First printing September 2015
978-0-9961346-0-6
10987654321

Dedication

To God be the glory! Everything else is secondary.

I am thankful for my mother, for the love of my life, Terrance Williamson, for my babies: Gabe, JJ, Jazz and JD. To my late granny, my brothers: Alfonso, CJ and Keyon, and my sister Nichelle. My mentor, Dr. Rosie Milligan, and Levester "Crunchie Munchie" Williams—I can never thank you enough, and to my friends who helped me walk this path.

The Lord has placed a lot of great people in my life to make this book come alive, especially LaTonya Patterson and Ashley Williams.

Who is the man, Jesus, you keep talking about?

It's early and Bible study seems to be really loud, as the youth ask the teacher lots of questions. Bible study is full of happiness and inspiration, as the children draw pictures of the great Savior Jesus Christ.

Communion is a serious part of the service for the adults, but the children's church is filled with workshops, Bible trivia and coloring pages of the stories in the Bible and the leaders who have shared their stories.

The coloring pages and the poetry that the children created are amazing. They wrote about our savior Jesus Christ. In the drawings he seems so huge. He looks so strong and mighty as he flies high over the church house and into the clouds. Every picture seems to display the leadership of Jesus and his teaching ability.

Class ends and a few little boys remain in their seats, holding their hands high in the air!

After Bible study, Jay asks Mama a deep question. "Mama, can you please tell me who is this man Jesus that we keep talking about and why haven't I ever seen Him before?"

Mama smiles. "Well, Jay, Jesus is the Son of God and…"

Jay is a bit confused. "Well, aren't I His son, too?"

Mama laughs and responds, "Of course you are His son, but Jesus was called on by God to die for our sins, son!"

Jay looks devastated.

"Mom, did Jesus die?"

Mom pats her little boy's head and lifts his chin, so she could look her baby firm in the eye. "He died and He returned home to save all of God's beautiful children!"

Mama takes Jay by his tiny hand and walks with him further into the forest.

"Mama, did Jesus save everyone?"

Nodding her head in agreement, Mama answers, "Jay, Jesus saved us all! He saved the people, all the animals, and the plants. He saved us all!"

Jay was excited. He nearly jumped out his skin as the bird seemed to overhear the conversation and rest on the end of the tree stump close by.

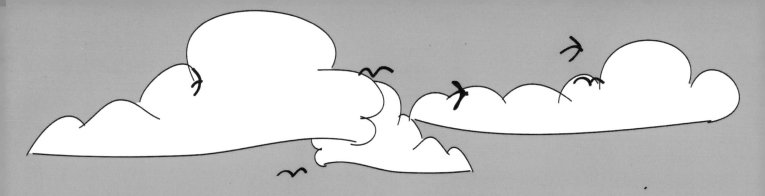

Jay scans the forest! He notices the rainbow in the sky, the speckles of the flowers, the hefty bushes, the sway of the breeze and, for the first time, he feels something is present that he has never laid his eyes on!

His mother's words of wisdom echoed in his head.

"Mom, why do I feel so funny inside when you talk about Jesus?"

With much enthusiasm, she lifts her heavy hands high in the air, showers her arms around the sky and directs her son to witness the demonstration.

Jay watched in amazement, as his mama hands flowed and swayed in the air!

"Son, Jesus is like the wind! You know it's there, but you can't see it!"

That is so awesome, Jay thought to himself. What If Jesus was like the wind—really like the wind, then He could be everywhere. Travel throughout walls, tunnels, in time, space! He can be tall as a tree and fast as a cheetah, fly high as a bird and grow as tiny as an ant! This man, Jesus—I guess the feeling inside me is right!

Jay's eyes were struck as he stared at the bird wandering the area around him.

Jay went to bed, dreaming of how great his next Sunday school class session will be!

"Yes, Jesus will be there, too!" he said to himself.

About the Author

Andrea was born in Los Angeles, California. She was the first in her family to graduate college. She earned a Master of Science degree in Entertainment Business from Full Sail University, as well as a Bachelor of Arts degree in Mass Media Arts from Clark Atlanta University. Andrea's writings have appeared in *Look Magazine*, *Sable Sportsman Magazine*, the *Explorer Newspaper*, the *Maroon Tiger Newspaper*, the *Panther Newspaper* and several others. She made her debut as a playwright with the production of "To Tell the Truth," which was featured in the 2011 NAACP Theatre Festival. In spring 2004, Andrea was featured in the "Life & Style" section of the *Atlanta Journal Constitution Newspaper* for participating in a forum with V-103 FM radio station and the Center for Disease Control at Clark Atlanta University to raise awareness for HIV/AIDS. She has four children and currently resides in Los Angeles, California.

About the Illustrator

Titus Rowell was born in North Carolina, but raised in Georgia. He graduated from the Art Institute of Atlanta, with a focus in Animation. Titus has a daughter that he holds dear to his heart and he also loves to play video games, watch cartoons and read comic books. Titus believes that you can never be too old for cartoons and super heroes. His favorite super hero is Spider-man. Titus currently resides in Atlanta, Georgia.

CPSIA information can be obtained at www.ICGtesting.com
Printed in the USA
LVIW01n0523071115
461355LV00007B/34